Growing Up
on Guam

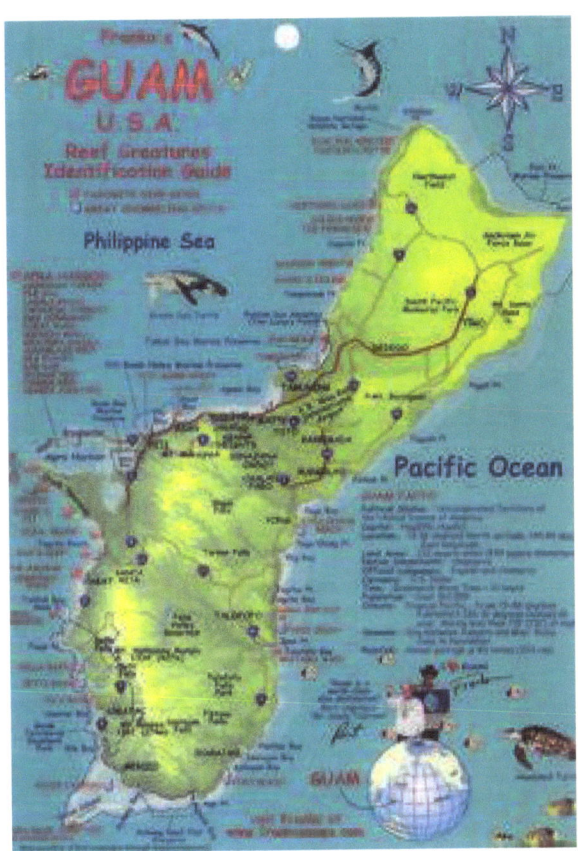

Childhood Memories
of Living on Guam

by Cherry Carl

Contents

Post War Guam

Since our dad was in the U.S. Navy when I was a little girl, my two sisters and I never knew what kind of adventures were just around the corner.

We lived on post-war Guam for a couple of years right after the Korean War and just seven years after WWII had ended. The Japanese military had captured and occupied Guam during most of that war and had eventually been defeated by U.S forces, and the island was recaptured. Even in 1953, eight years after the war, you could see evidence of the Japanese having been there and occupying the island. Along with the giant African snails they brought to Guam, we saw munitions and unexploded bombs in the jungle between our house and the beach and some in the jungle surrounding Adelup Point School. On the waterfront was a concrete Japanese pillbox that was built as a coastal defense during the war. Since this was on the western side of the island, there was not much left after the destruction by invading allied forces. There was no roof left, and the windows were just large square openings. Large guns had originally been placed by the Japanese in the gun ports facing out to the unknown enemy in the sea. The Agana-Hagåtña Pillbox north of Agat is listed on the National Register of Historic Places and is seen as part of a walking tour of the area. There are three more pillboxes further north on or near the beach of Tumon Bay. The Pago Bay pillboxes are located on the east coast of Guam and can be seen today, partly because they saw limited action during the 1944 liberation of Guam and partly because of their location.

According to Wikipedia, Agat was one of the two landing sites for the U.S. Marines. The old village of Agat was destroyed during the invasion and reconstructed by the U.S. military for Guam residents made homeless by the war. It was built just south of the original village, and by the time we arrived eight years later, it was a thriving community with a church and a school for the village children and a commissioner by the name of Antonio P. Carbullido, our friendly neighbor and landlord.

Mr. Carbullido and his family included us in a family celebration. There was a table that seemed to be about 20 foot long and it was loaded with food, some that I had never seen or tasted before. Pork, chicken, and seafood were the main dishes and served with rice and an endless variety of fresh fruit. I remember walking from one end of the table to the other, speculating about the identity of some foods. I decided to only eat what I recognized. One strange-looking dish was octopus, but I wasn't brave enough to try that!

Growing Up in Agat, Guam

One of the most exciting experiences we had was when we moved to that small, sunny tropical island in the Pacific Ocean. Daddy was already there, waiting for us to join him. His military orders had sent him to Guam several months before military housing was available for the rest of us. Daddy hated being on Guam by himself while we were left in San Diego, waiting for a place to live and a ship to take us to him. He took it upon himself to find housing for us so that we could join him.

In early August, my mother and my two sisters, and I traveled by train to San Francisco. I can't imagine what my mother went through all by herself, pushing a stroller by herself up the hills in San Francisco on the way to the pier. I remember that she made sure that we were all dressed appropriately and presented ourselves as the well-behaved young ladies she was teaching us to be. She even wore high-heeled shoes. My baby sister, Katie, lost one of her shiny new shoes somewhere in the streets of San Francisco.

On August 11, 1953, we sailed out of San Francisco, California, on the USNS General D.E. Aultman. It had been a navy ship that was later turned over to the Merchant Marine services. It was ill-equipped to carry Mama and three little girls. There were a few other families on the ship, but I don't remember being allowed to play with them. But my older sister, Lydia, remembers things that I have no memory of. For instance, the ship had a laundry area for families to use, and it even had irons and ironing boards. Mama was ironing our clothes (no permanent press in those days), and my youngest sister, Katie, wanted her attention, so she pulled the cord to the iron. Mama caught the iron with her open hand. If she hadn't, it would have landed on Katie's face. That is when Lydia learned how to iron!

It was a long and lonely three-week trip since the crew members were too busy to spend time with us, and there was nothing to keep us entertained. Mama resorted to teaching Lydia and I how to play canasta.

There was no ship's store for Mama to replenish essential supplies so when Katie, our baby sister, broke her last glass baby bottle on the way, she took to sucking her thumb for comfort instead! Poor baby!

During our long and boring voyage (eighteen days), we went through a hurricane at sea, and I am sure we were all seasick and confined to our rooms for safety's sake. We were very thankful to reach Guam, no matter what kind of home Daddy had managed to find for us. My sisters and I thought it was an awesome adventure, but

Mama was sure she was living through a nightmare in that old tub of a boat!

We finally sailed into Guam's harbor in the middle of the night and soon found ourselves in Agat, a village inhabited by the native Chamorros and one American family, the Olivers (us). It was the only place on the island that had a house to rent. When we walked across the yard to the front door, something crunched loudly under our feet. We could not see what it was in the dark, but in the morning light, we saw that the crunching sound was made from walking over a yard full of giant African snails! My understanding was that the Japanese occupation troops had imported them as a delicacy for their dining pleasure during their three-year occupation of the island during World War II from 1941 to 1944. Their shells were large and thick, and a broken shell could pierce a tire, and we heard blowouts in the middle of the night that sounded like gunfire. Of course, tires in those days and in that location were nothing compared to what we have today. (Military vehicles were equipped with far better tires than the cars owned by villagers.)

The house that we lived in was built high above the ground. It had a tin roof that leaked whenever it rained and a wooden floor with knotholes in it. You could count on it to rain every afternoon, and so our new home, and everything in it, was very wet at first. Mama never gave up, and she did not run out of ideas! She nailed tin can lids over all the open knotholes in the floor to keep the geckos and enormous spiders out. Since we lived in a wet, tropical climate, she had to keep our food in plastic so that it did not turn green and fuzzy from mold! (See Three Cheers for Tupperware!) Most of our food came from the commissary and was in tin cans, Spam and salmon being two of Daddy's favorites. I think we ate one of the two for dinner each week after that until I left for college. I still don't care for salmon croquettes to this day!

My worst memory of living in that house in Agat was what the humidity did to our one and only shower. Like most showers on the island, they were constructed of concrete (no pretty tile there!). The walls of the shower were slimy, and so was the floor. Slipping was a hazard, and we all had to wear what we called "shower shoes." These days, we call them flip-flops. Anyway, one evening, Mama told me to go and take a shower. When I pulled back the shower curtain, I was greeted by the sight of an enormous spider on the wall at about eye level. I whined and complained to Mama, but she said that the spider would not bother me. I hate to admit that I solved my dilemma by being a naughty girl. I turned on the shower water, washed myself in the bathroom sink and then turned the shower off, figuring that enough time had lapsed for Mama to believe I took my shower. I am sorry to say that I never told her what I really did.

We had an exciting experience one evening when our new neighbor's wife began to scream at the top of her lungs. Daddy, being the hero type, believed that the husband was abusing his wife and ran over there to rescue her. His help wasn't needed, because the cause of her screaming was the gecko that fell from the ceiling and right into the front of her blouse! There was a lot of giggling at my house that night!

Lydia always took the lead in our little trio of sisters and was a big help to Mama when she had to have thyroid surgery while we lived in Agat. We had an old wringer-type washing machine, and Lydia did the laundry while Mama was recuperating from her operation. She remembers getting her arm caught in the wringer. Daddy had to take the wringer apart to rescue her, but she does not remember feeling any pain, and, fortunately, nothing was broken!

Agat experienced blackouts once a month because military patrols were still looking for Japanese soldiers hiding in the jungle. "Sergeant Shoichi Yokoi, who surrendered in January 1972, appears to have been the last confirmed holdout, having held out for 28 years in the forested back country on Guam." (Wikipedia) He was sent home, reunited with his family, got married and came back to Guam for his honeymoon!

I had my eighth birthday in that funny little house. It was a stormy night, of course, when we sat down to enjoy my birthday dinner. Mama was ready to light the candles, but . . . plop, plop, plop! It rained on the table! We moved that tiny table around the house, and every time we stopped, the rain made another plop, plop, plopping sound! We finally found a dry dining spot in their bedroom!

For many years, my family laughed about the endless rain on the island of Guam. When Lydia and I were teenagers and asked Daddy if we could do something, instead of saying, "Maybe," or "No," he always said, "Sure, when it snows on Guam!" Right!

There's a Big Green Monster
Under the Bed!

When Daddy first rented the shack of a home for us in Agat, there were three little beds in the room that Lydia and I shared with our younger sister, Katie. They reminded me of Papa, Mama, and Baby Bear beds. Daddy was so tired that first night that he sat down on the side of one of the beds to take his dress shoes off, and he put them under the bed. Apparently, he forgot about those shoes and kept asking Mama to bring his dress shoes with her when she packed for the trip to Guam. She kept telling him that they were not in San Diego. Weeks later, when we arrived, Mama went in to make up the beds for three weary little girls and came out screaming, "Paul, there's something large and green and furry under one of the beds!" It was Daddy's size 12 leather dress shoes, covered in mold, and that would scare anybody!

School Days

My sister, Lydia, and I were soon enrolled in the only school on the island provided by the military, Adelup Point Elementary School. I was in the second grade, and Lydia was in the third grade. The first morning, we took the bus to school and were astonished to see the parking lot was a sea of big, yellow numbered buses. Military enlisted men were the drivers and aides who maintained order during the trip to the school. At the end of the day, we all trooped out to the parking lot to board the buses for the return trip home. I was terrified that I would get on the wrong bus since they all looked alike. I was just about ready to burst into tears, and frantically looking for my sister when she appeared and led me to the right bus.

Every school has its own set of rules for the classroom, and Adelup was no different. We were not allowed to leave the room during instruction, even if we needed to use the restroom. I was mortified one day when my weak bladder betrayed me during class, leaving a large wet spot on the concrete floor. I think that's why I never refused a request to use the restroom during my 35 years of teaching!

It's A Giant Pillbox!

Lydia and I explored the deserted Japanese pillbox on the beach across the road after the morning tide had washed in a plethora of starfish, crabs, and sand dollars. The floor of the pillbox consisted of coral and limestone, so it was common for us to come home with scratches from the coral. One of us found a giant conch shell, and that thing traveled with us for decades and acted as a doorstop in our homes between Guam and Pennsylvania and back to San Diego. Its final resting place is somewhere in Arkansas, where Daddy took the family after he retired from the Navy.

Katie was too young to go with us when we explored the beach. Believe me, Mama had to keep a close eye on her since she could disappear in an instant. We would often find her in the bushes eating brown seeds, and we just had to follow the crunching sound to find her. Thank goodness they were not poisonous! Before we left Guam, Lydia bought Chamorro gifts for me and for Mama. They were long necklaces and bracelets made of those very same brown seeds.

We didn't dare go into the jungle on either side of the dirt path to the beach because you really couldn't be sure of what or who might be in there. At night, the wild dogs that were left by the Japanese would roam the island looking for prey like chickens and pigs and such. You could hear them coming up the road, barking and growling and snarling at each other. As soon as the sun went down in the early evenings, the Guamanians would move their livestock into safety, and Daddy warned us about being outside at night. Sometimes, being a perfect example of an obstinate and willful toddler, Katie often refused to come inside when Mama called her to come into the house, day or night. When we were called to come in from playing together, Lydia and I came right away, but we could see the bushes moving to indicate that a small child was in there. Daddy resorted to making the snorting sound of Mr. Carbullido's rather large hog, and that always sent her scurrying inside. Lydia reminded me that there were also scary wild pigs roaming about after dark.

Three Cheers for Tupperware!

We probably would have starved to death if Mama had left her precious Tupperware in San Diego. Even though they were and still are rather bulky containers to pack, she insisted that she was not leaving home without them! You see, Guam's humidity destroyed most anything she kept in our cupboards, and mold grew everywhere and on everything. Commodities were scarce on the island because they had to come from the mainland on slowly moving commercial ships. The Tupperware containers preserved dry products like flour, salt, and cornmeal so that Mama could at least bake biscuits and cornbread for our southern Mississippi daddy. I do believe that she still had some of her favorite pieces from Guam in her cupboard when she died. What a testament to the endurance of Tupperware!

Lydia's worst memory of any kind of beverage on Guam was the fact that the only milk we could get was frozen. Can you imagine drinking thawed buttermilk? Until then, she loved drinking buttermilk with Daddy, just like any good southern girl, but the way it separated upon being thawed killed any desire for another glass! I seem to remember powdered milk that had to be kept in sealed containers to preserve it. When I was a teen and we were living out in the country, my parents had three goats. My mother milked them daily and mixed their milk with powdered milk to extend the family budget. I hated powdered milk then, and I still do!

Lydia also vividly remembers something in the kitchen in Agat that I don't remember at all. She swears that the house had something like a food safe, and since it was airtight, mold and mildew did not have access to the food stored inside.

Swapping Sandwiches

There was an abundance of banana trees in the yard of our tropical Agat home. Our landlord, Mr. Carbullido, was a real sweetheart and would always chop down a whole banana stalk to hang on our back porch so that they would ripen enough to eat. Apparently, banana growers do not usually wait for them to ripen on the trees but harvest them when they are about 75% mature. As a result, we had as many bananas as we could eat. One day, Mama decided that she would not wait for Mr. Carbullido and tried to cut a stalk down herself. She got a strong lecture from him about using the enormous machete and the possibility of losing an arm or a leg! Nevertheless, she wasn't successful in her efforts, and even though she barely understood the scolding in his native Chamorro language about bees and bananas, she got the message and never tried it again. The worst part about it was being chased into the house and stung by a bunch of angry bees while Daddy just laughed and said, "I told you so!"

Mama made scrumptious salads for family feasts with the native fruits that flourished in the island's tropical climate. These included bananas, papayas, coconuts, mangoes, and dozens more that were readily available for picking and/or purchase in local markets.

Peanut butter and banana sandwiches were what we could look forward to every day because that is what Mama usually packed in our school lunches! Lydia remembers that once a month, when supply ships came in, we got a package of baloney. Mama also managed to make cream cheese and black olive sandwiches. (Lydia's granddaughter, Kylie, says that sounds good, like a tea sandwich.)

One of Lydia's classmates was the governor's grandson, and he had gourmet lunches that were prepared and packed by the chef in his Grandpa's kitchen. However, he did not want those delicious ham and cheese sandwiches. He wanted peanut butter and banana or peanut butter and jelly, so he swapped lunches with Lydia every day! As I recall, Elvis Presley was a Mississippi boy like Daddy and loved peanut butter and banana sandwiches, too. Must be in the genes!

Mother Nature's Bad Mood

There are only two events from my early life that come close to some of the clips we see today in the weather reports from battered coastal cities around the world.

The first event happened while living through a typhoon in that quiet seaside village on the island of Guam when I was eight years old. The shack-like house we lived in was right across the road from the beach, and if we walked down a dirt path, we'd come to the beach, which we frequently did in the afternoons so Mama could paint endless sunsets while we collected seashells. We were that close to the ocean, not a place to be in the path of a typhoon.

The morning of the approaching typhoon, Mama put my sister and I on the military school bus that picked us up and took us along the coastal road to Adelup Point, to the school for the children of military families. When we came to the first bridge crossing, we saw that it had been washed out, and we had to turn around and go back home. We saw many domestic animals that belonged to our village friends floating out to sea, carried along in the turbulent, muddy water.

Mama was standing on the porch waiting for us, and I found myself waist-deep in the mucky water when I stepped off the bus. One of the bus attendants rushed to my rescue and carried me to the house. Fortunately, Lydia was tall enough to make her way by herself.

Mama brought us into the house to dry us off and get cleaned up, but that was never going to happen. You see, the tin roof leaked like a sieve. That was not the only problem we faced by any stretch of the imagination.

Mama was wading in ankle-deep water in the living room when we got home, and so she pried up a bunch of tin can lids covering the knotholes. To my young mind, it sounded like a giant bathtub draining! We were, of course, immediately inundated with all those creepy crawly things trying to escape certain death by drowning below the house.

We were not home for long when Daddy arrived to move us to higher ground in the hills. Because of the typhoon, there was a warning of a tidal wave created by the storm surge. He took us to a friend's quarters up in the hills. The tidal wave? It never happened, but what a day for Mother Nature to be in a grumpy mood!

Some people might wonder why we were living in such disheveled surroundings, but we went to Guam before military housing was available for all the arriving families.

Note: I looked online while writing this and discovered that Adelup Point Elementary School is still there and in use! We went to school there in 1953 and 1954 and had to stay on campus the entire day because there was live ammo in the surrounding jungle and probably still is. Do the math and figure out how long ago that was! Better yet, do a Google search for Adelup Point Elementary School and watch the beautiful video about the history of the school.

Earthquake!

What happened the second time Mother Nature shook us up? Guam is a volcanic island, and so we experienced lots of rumbling and grumbling from beneath our feet. However, my most vivid memory happened when we were finally able to move into a Quonset hut, which was the U.S. military's answer to family housing.

One of the drawbacks of living there was the nightly curfew when all residents were required to stay indoors. Large trucks came through the community and sprayed pesticide to fumigate the area and prevent mosquitoes. I recently read an article that claims that Agent Orange was used on Japanese soldiers on Guam during the Korean War. That is not a happy thought, especially since Daddy was near the Bikini Atoll during testing of the nuclear bomb and exposed to the hazards of that event. It also makes me wonder what was in the soil we played in, and around the island and that produced the fresh produce we consumed while we were there.

While living in the Quonset hut community, Lydia had a school friend by the name of Leilani Miller, an only child of an officer on base. They played together after school and frequently spent time on the beach below the housing. Lydia remembers the day they were digging in the sand and unearthed a bundle of sealed C-Rations (she called them C-Rats). Everything inside was sealed, and so they opened and ate the tin of cookies. I guess they were afraid to try any of the other food items. The only reasonable explanation for those C-Rations being there was that when the military recaptured the island from the Japanese, they landed on the beach in that area as well as on Agat Beach. Someone lost them, and it took two curious little girls to find them.

The military housing had a small church down the hill from our Quonset hut home. The pastor was a navy officer by the name of Chaplain E.L. Wade, and we loved attending Sunday school and church there. Mama sang in the choir, and everyone loved to hear her sing. We had several good friends in Sunday school, and years later, when I was teaching school, I realized that I was living right across the street from one of those girls. We had even attended the same high school in San Diego. We renewed our friendship and enjoyed many good times together for years to come. It is amazing how many times our paths crossed as teens and adults. What a small world!

My sister, Lydia, and I shared a bedroom on one side of the small apartment of the Quonset hut with Katie, and we were separated from our parents by the living room and kitchen while they had a bedroom on the far side of the hut. Our tiny room had a crib for Katie and twin beds for Lydia and I. Mine was next to the far wall when a large and lengthy earthquake hit in the middle of the night, our room was like a roller coaster in motion! My bed moved across the room, but not before dropping me onto the floor, and then rolling back over me. I don't know how, but I slept through the entire thing. What woke me up was Mama's screams that "Cherry Anne has disappeared with the earthquake!"

It is no wonder that I have always had a deep-seated, lifelong fear of earthquakes. Living near the San Andreas fault in southern California years later certainly did not help! You just can't get away from Mother Nature!

Pretty Pink Panties

Speaking of being scarce, pink panties, or any color for that matter, were nonexistent on Guam in the military stores, but Mama was determined that we were going to have them, even if it meant making them herself. She found pink cotton cloth somewhere and got busy making her version of "designer" panties. She did not own a sewing machine until we moved to Philadelphia after our return to the States, so she must have sewn these by hand. It was like wearing bloomers from the roaring twenties! I hated those things, especially with all the bulges the elastic made beneath our skirts. Oh, well, her heart was in the right place. It was better than no panties! However, I ruined one pair when I was playing hide and seek with my sisters. I backed into a protruding nail on the Quonset hut, and I still have the scar on my hip to prove it!

The Farewell Tour

Daddy wanted us to see more of Guam before leaving for his next assignment in the States, so he took us on a tour of the island, which has an area of 210 square miles. Yes, we had transportation, a well-used car that had been passed from sailor to sailor, but we never really had the opportunity to get around much while we lived there. We saw more dense jungle on that day trip than I think I will ever see in my lifetime, and that noisy old car was sold to the next incoming sailor.

Daddy told us the story of his Navy friend, George Ray Tweed, a Radioman First Class, who had escaped capture by the invading forces during WWII and survived in that jungle for two years and seven months before being rescued by the Americans. The natives helped him by supplying food and shelter. He later wrote a book about his adventure called "Robinson Crusoe,

U.S.N." Our family has a signed copy of the book, and it is quite a captivating tale of his adventures and of those who helped him survive.

One of the places we saw that day was called Magellan Fort, named after the Portuguese navigator who was the first European to visit Guam in 1521. Ferdinand Magellan was sailing for the King of Spain, and Guam was later claimed by Spain in 1565 and colonized around 1668. They brought Christianity and the Catholic church to the island, and that influence remains to this day. In the little village of Agat, about a block away from our home, was a Catholic compound with a large church and a Catholic school for the village children.

I remember Daddy driving around a large mud hole where a large water buffalo or carabao was contentedly chewing her cud as if to say, "Don't bother me."

Hello U.S.A.!

I don't remember when we left Guam to come back to the mainland, but Lydia seems to think we were there for eighteen months, which would put our departure taking place in February of 1955. We sailed back on a beautiful ocean liner, and the trip only took eleven days. This ship was fully air-conditioned, unlike the one that took us to Guam. However, most of us were very seasick on the way home. I remember Mama and Daddy trying, to no avail, to get me to eat something in the large dining room. I spent most of the trip in my bunk and only felt well when we could go up on deck into the fresh air.

The ship took us to San Francisco, and once we arrived, Daddy immediately went to buy a new car so we could drive to San Diego. He bought a new two-tone Plymouth, and it was probably the only time in his life that he bought a new car! I don't remember anything about that drive. Lydia just remembers the fun of getting big rig truck drivers to honk their horns.

The best part about coming back to San Diego was the fact that we no longer had to use intensive mosquito repellent every night. When we lived in that little house in Agat, we were perpetually invaded by swarms of mosquitoes inside and out because of the many flaws in construction. It was almost as if we extended an open invitation to them. Daddy sprayed our bedrooms with what we all called mosquito bombs, cylindrical metal containers with end caps. He unscrewed the cap before bedtime, allowing the mist to permeate the room. One night, he dropped the cap on the floor and by the time he had retrieved it and put it back on the bomb, the air was toxic, making it difficult to breathe. As a result, we had to sleep on the floor in our parents' bedroom. When we went into our bedroom the next morning, the ceiling was green from the spray. I'm sure that procedure and repellent would be illegal now and could possibly have been a cancer hazard.

Appendix

Passenger list for our 18-day trip to Guam
aboard the USNS General D.E. Aultman

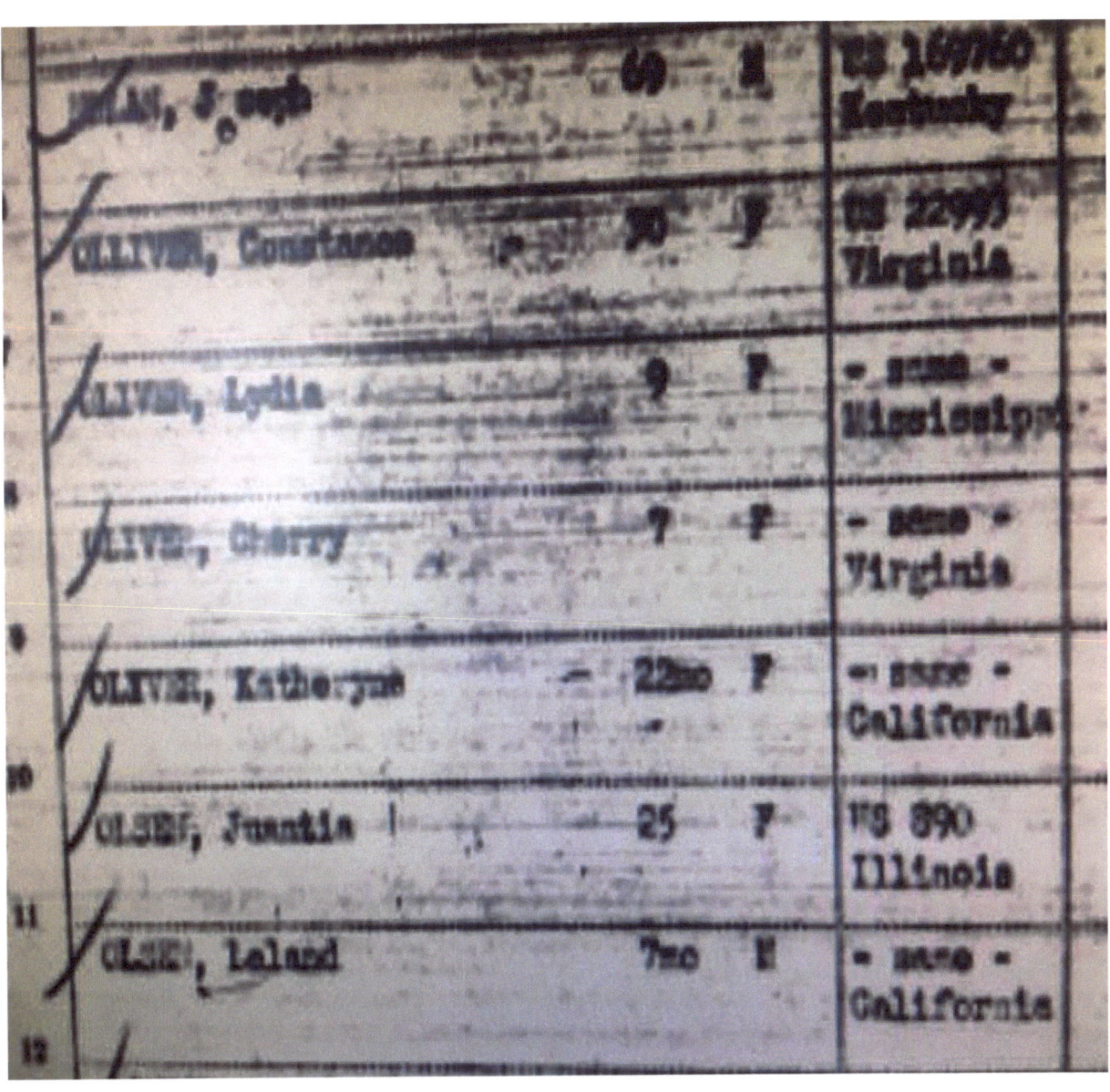

Magellan Point

Japanese Pillbox Near Agat Beach

Cherry and Katie on Quonset Hut Steps

Mama and Katie on Guam Picnic

Katie and Her Beau at the Beach

The Three Sisters Sail to the USA

Day's End at Agat Beach